LINKEDIN MARKETING SCHOOL

LINKEDIN MARKETING SCHOOL

HAROLD BROCK

First Printing, 2025

Contents

1

Getting Started with LinkedIn

In today's digital age, social media platforms have revolutionized the way we connect, network, and market ourselves and our businesses. Among the myriad of platforms available, LinkedIn stands out as a powerful tool specifically designed for professionals. With its vast network of over 740 million users spanning various industries and sectors, LinkedIn offers unparalleled opportunities for business growth, personal branding, and professional networking.

Chapter 1 will guide you through the process of getting started with LinkedIn, from setting up a professional profile to identifying your target audience. But before we dive into the practical steps, let's explore what LinkedIn is, why you should be using it, and the advantages it holds for your business.

LinkedIn is a social media platform tailored to professionals, serving as a virtual hub for career development, industry insights, and business connections. It goes beyond traditional job search platforms and serves as a comprehensive ecosystem where professionals can showcase their expertise, engage with like-minded individuals, and leverage their networks to unlock new opportunities.

So, why should you be using LinkedIn for your business? Here are a few compelling reasons:

1. *Professional Networking:* LinkedIn provides a platform for connecting with col-

leagues, peers, industry influencers, and potential clients or customers. It allows you to expand your professional network, nurture relationships, and tap into a vast pool of industry expertise and knowledge.

2. *Personal Branding:* LinkedIn offers a unique opportunity to establish and strengthen your personal brand. By crafting a compelling profile, sharing thought-provoking content, and engaging in industry discussions, you can position yourself as an authority in your field and gain credibility within your professional community.
3. *Business Visibility:* LinkedIn enables you to showcase your company's products, services, and achievements through a dedicated company page. It serves as a digital storefront, allowing you to reach a wide audience, engage with followers, and attract potential customers or clients.
4. *Industry Insights and Learning:* LinkedIn provides access to a wealth of industry-specific content, discussions, and thought

leadership. By following relevant influencers, joining industry groups, and participating in discussions, you can stay up-to-date with the latest trends, gain valuable insights, and expand your knowledge base.

5. *Recruitment and Talent Acquisition:* LinkedIn is widely used by recruiters and hiring managers to identify and connect with potential candidates. By maintaining an active presence on LinkedIn, you can attract top talent, explore career opportunities, and stay connected with the evolving job market.

As we delve into Chapter 1, we will explore the essential steps to harness the power of LinkedIn for your business. From setting up a professional profile that highlights your skills and achievements to identifying your target audience and laying the groundwork for effective marketing strategies, you will gain the necessary knowledge and tools to navigate the world of LinkedIn with confidence.

So, let's embark on this journey together and unlock the boundless possibilities that LinkedIn offers to market your business, establish your professional brand, and connect with a thriving professional community.

Setting up a Professional LinkedIn Profile

Your LinkedIn profile is the foundation of your online presence on the platform. It serves as your digital resume and a powerful tool for personal branding. Here are the key steps to set up a professional LinkedIn profile:

1. *Choose a Professional Profile Picture:* Select a high-quality headshot that portrays you in a professional and approachable manner. Dress appropriately for your industry and ensure a clean background.
2. *Craft a Compelling Headline:* Your headline appears below your name and is a prime opportunity to showcase your exper-

tise and value proposition. Use keywords relevant to your industry and role.

3. *Create a Captivating Summary:* Write a concise and engaging summary that highlights your professional background, skills, achievements, and goals. Make it authentic and compelling to capture the attention of visitors.
4. *Showcase Your Experience:* Add your work experience, starting with your current or most recent position. Include relevant job titles, companies, responsibilities, and accomplishments. Use bullet points to make it easily scannable.
5. *Highlight Your Education and Certifications:* Include your educational background, degrees, certifications, and any relevant courses you have completed.
6. *Add Skills and Endorsements:* List your key skills, which will help others understand your areas of expertise. Encourage colleagues and connections to endorse you for these skills to boost credibility.

7. *Utilize the Featured Section:* LinkedIn offers a featured section where you can showcase samples of your work, articles, or projects. Leverage this section to provide evidence of your skills and accomplishments.
8. *Customize Your Public Profile URL:* Create a personalized URL for your LinkedIn profile to make it easier for others to find you. Use your name or a variation of it.

Identifying Your Target Audience on LinkedIn

Before you can effectively market your business on LinkedIn, it's crucial to identify and understand your target audience. LinkedIn offers a wealth of user data and targeting options that can help you connect with the right people. Here's how to identify your target audience on LinkedIn:

1. *Define Your Ideal Customer:* Start by creating a detailed profile of your ideal cus-

tomer or client. Consider factors such as demographics, job titles, industries, company size, and professional interests.

2. *Conduct Market Research:* Use LinkedIn's search filters and advanced search options to find professionals who fit your target audience criteria. Explore their profiles, connections, and engagement to gain insights into their interests and behaviors.
3. *Analyze Competitor Connections:* Explore the LinkedIn profiles of your competitors and analyze their connections. Look for commonalities and patterns to identify potential target audience segments.
4. *Leverage LinkedIn Groups:* Join relevant LinkedIn Groups in your industry or niche. Observe discussions, engage with members, and identify individuals who align with your target audience.
5. *Utilize LinkedIn Insights:* LinkedIn provides valuable insights and analytics on your company page, allowing you to understand the demographics, engagement lev-

els, and preferences of your followers. Use this data to refine your target audience.

6. *Refine Your Messaging:* Based on your research, tailor your messaging and content to resonate with your target audience. Speak their language, address their pain points, and offer solutions that are relevant to their needs.

By setting up a professional LinkedIn profile and identifying your target audience, you'll establish a solid foundation for leveraging LinkedIn's marketing capabilities to promote your business effectively.

2

Building your LinkedIn Network

In today's interconnected professional landscape, building a strong network is a fundamental aspect of success. LinkedIn, the world's leading professional networking platform, offers unparalleled opportunities to connect, engage, and collaborate with professionals from various industries and backgrounds. Chapter 2 will guide you through the strategies and techniques to build a robust LinkedIn network that can fuel your business growth, expand your knowledge base, and open doors to exciting professional opportunities.

Connecting with Colleagues and Peers

Your professional network is an extension of your real-life relationships, and LinkedIn provides a platform to strengthen and expand those connections. Whether they are current or former colleagues, classmates, or acquaintances, connecting with them on LinkedIn allows you to stay connected and tap into their professional expertise. By employing effective strategies to connect with colleagues and peers, you can cultivate a network that reflects your real-world relationships.

When it comes to connecting with colleagues and peers on LinkedIn, there are several key strategies you can implement to build and enhance your network:

1. *Import Contacts:* LinkedIn offers the option to import your contacts from various email providers. By importing your con-

tacts, you can quickly find and connect with colleagues, classmates, and professional acquaintances, expanding your network efficiently. This feature saves you time and ensures that you don't overlook potential connections.

2. *Personalize Connection Requests:* Sending personalized connection requests is vital to establishing meaningful connections. Take the time to customize each request, mentioning how you know the person or why you would like to connect. A personalized message shows that you value the relationship and increases the likelihood of acceptance. It helps you stand out from generic connection requests and sets the foundation for a more authentic connection.
3. *Engage with Current and Former Colleagues:* Seek out current and former colleagues on LinkedIn and connect with them. Engage with their posts, congratulate them on professional milestones, and maintain an active presence within your professional circle. These interactions con-

tribute to strengthening relationships and expanding your network's reach. By engaging with their content, you demonstrate your support and interest in their professional endeavors, fostering a sense of camaraderie.

4. *Attend Industry Events and Conferences:* LinkedIn is not limited to online connections alone. If you attend industry events or conferences, make an effort to connect with fellow attendees on LinkedIn. By forging connections with individuals you meet in person, you solidify the relationship and can continue engaging beyond the event. Attendees of industry events often share common interests and goals, making them valuable additions to your network.

5. *Participate in Alumni Networks:* Many educational institutions have dedicated alumni groups on LinkedIn. Joining these groups enables you to connect with fellow alumni, engage in discussions, and tap into a network of professionals who share a common educational background. Alumni

> connections often provide a strong foundation for professional collaboration and opportunities. By leveraging your alma mater's network, you can establish connections based on shared experiences and create meaningful relationships.

Building a network of colleagues and peers on LinkedIn is not merely about accumulating connections; it is about nurturing relationships and fostering a supportive community. By actively engaging with your connections, staying connected with current and former colleagues, and leveraging in-person events and alumni networks, you can develop a robust professional network that serves as a valuable resource throughout your career journey.

Engaging with Industry Influencers and Thought Leaders

LinkedIn offers a unique opportunity to connect and engage with influential figures and thought leaders within your industry. These individuals possess a wealth of knowledge, share valuable insights, and shape industry conversations. By actively engaging with industry influencers, you can expand your own knowledge, gain visibility, and tap into their networks.

To effectively engage with industry influencers and thought leaders on LinkedIn, consider the following strategies:

1. *Follow Influencers:* Identify prominent figures in your industry and follow them on LinkedIn. Influencers often share valuable insights, industry news, and thought-provoking content. By following them, you can stay informed, gain inspiration, and enhance your own content creation. Additionally, their posts may spark discussions and provide opportunities for meaningful engagement.
2. *Engage with Influencer Content:* Regularly engage with the content shared by influencers. Like, comment, and share their posts to show your support and contribute

to the conversation. Thoughtful engagement helps you build relationships and increases your visibility within their networks. When commenting, provide insights or ask thoughtful questions that demonstrate your knowledge and genuine interest in the topic.

3. *Contribute to Discussions:* Actively participate in discussions within LinkedIn groups, posts, and articles. Share your expertise, ask questions, and provide valuable insights. Meaningful participation in discussions allows you to showcase your industry knowledge, establish yourself as a thought leader, and attract the attention of industry influencers. Engaging in discussions fosters connections with like-minded professionals and expands your network beyond direct connections.
4. *Collaborate on Content:* Seek opportunities to collaborate with industry influencers and thought leaders on content creation. This could include co-authoring articles, participating in podcasts, or being

featured in interviews. Collaborative content allows you to tap into their audience and expand your reach. It also positions you as an expert in your field and provides credibility through association with influential figures.

5. *Attend Webinars and Virtual Events:* Many industry influencers and thought leaders host webinars and virtual events on LinkedIn. Participate in these events, ask questions, and connect with attendees. It's an excellent opportunity to learn, network, and establish connections with influential individuals. By actively engaging in these virtual events, you can gain insights, make valuable connections, and contribute to the professional conversations happening within your industry.

Engaging with industry influencers and thought leaders requires a proactive approach. By following influencers, engaging with their content, participating in discussions, collaborating on content, and attending virtual events, you position yourself as a knowledgeable and engaged professional within your industry. These engagements can lead to opportunities for mentorship, collaboration, and exposure to new ideas and trends.

3

Creating an Effective LinkedIn Profile

Your LinkedIn profile is your digital representation in the professional world. It serves as a powerful tool to showcase your skills, experience, and personal brand. In Chapter 3, we will explore the key elements and strategies for creating an effective LinkedIn profile that attracts attention, establishes credibility, and helps you stand out in a competitive market. By optimizing your profile, you can maximize your visibility, expand your network, and create opportunities for business growth and career advancement.

Creating an impactful LinkedIn profile involves attention to detail and careful consideration of various components. Let's dive into the essential elements that make up an effective LinkedIn profile.

Profile Photo and Background Image

Your profile photo is the first impression you make on LinkedIn, and it should convey professionalism and approachability. When selecting a profile photo, choose a high-quality image where you are dressed appropriately for your industry. A friendly smile can help create a welcoming impression. Additionally, consider using a background image that aligns with your personal brand or showcases your professional interests. It adds visual interest to your profile and further reflects your personality and industry focus.

Compelling Headline

Your headline appears just below your name and is a prime opportunity to grab attention. Instead of simply stating your job title, craft a compelling headline that highlights your unique value proposition and captures the interest of visitors. Use concise and impactful language to communicate your expertise, industry focus, and professional goals. A compelling headline helps you stand out among other professionals and entices visitors to learn more about you.

Summary Statement

The summary section is your chance to tell your professional story and provide a comprehensive overview of your background, skills, and career aspirations. It should be concise, engaging, and focused on highlighting your key achievements and areas of expertise. Use this section to showcase your unique value proposition, convey your passion for your work, and demonstrate your commitment to excellence. A well-crafted summary statement can pique the interest of visitors and compel them to explore further.

Experience and Achievements

The experience section allows you to showcase your professional journey, including your current and past roles, responsibilities, and accomplishments. Use bullet points or concise paragraphs to outline your key achievements, highlighting the quantifiable impact you made in each role. Incorporate relevant keywords to optimize your profile for searchability within your industry. Additionally, consider adding multimedia elements such as links to projects, articles, or presentations to provide further evidence of your expertise.

Skills and Endorsements

LinkedIn provides a dedicated section for listing your skills. Choose skills that align with your industry, expertise, and career goals. Be specific and include both hard and soft skills. Prioritize skills that are most relevant to your current objectives. As you grow your network, actively seek endorsements from colleagues, clients, and other professionals. Endorsements validate your skills and enhance your profile's credibility.

Recommendations

Recommendations are powerful social proof of your professional abilities and character. Reach out to colleagues, supervisors, clients, and other professional connections and kindly request recommendations. Provide them with guidance on what aspects you would like them to highlight in their recommendation. Positive recommendations strengthen your profile and enhance your professional reputation.

Education and Certifications

Include your educational background, highlighting relevant degrees, certifications, and courses. Mention any honors, awards, or notable achievements during your academic journey. This section demonstrates your commitment to continuous learning and development, adding depth to your professional profile.

Additional Sections and Media

LinkedIn offers additional sections where you can showcase your publications, volunteer experiences, languages spoken, and other relevant information. Take advantage of these sections to provide a more comprehensive overview of your professional background and interests. Additionally, leverage multimedia elements such as images, videos, or presentations to enrich your profile and make it visually engaging.

Engaging with Content

An effective LinkedIn profile is not just a static representation; it's a platform for engagement. Actively participate in discussions, share valuable content, and contribute insights within your industry.

Engaging with content helps you build relationships, expand your network, and position yourself as a knowledgeable professional within your field.

By optimizing each element of your LinkedIn profile, you can create a compelling digital presence that captures attention and showcases your professional brand. Invest time in crafting a well-written summary, highlight your achievements, and seek endorsements and recommendations to strengthen your profile's credibility. Remember to engage with content and leverage multimedia elements to provide a dynamic and visually appealing profile.

4

Creating Engaging Content on LinkedIn

Content is king, and on LinkedIn, creating engaging and valuable content is key to attracting attention, building your brand, and fostering meaningful connections. In Chapter 4, we will delve into the strategies and techniques for creating compelling content on LinkedIn that resonates with your target audience and helps you achieve your business objectives. By mastering the art of content creation, you can establish yourself as a thought leader, expand your reach, and drive business growth.

Understanding Your Target Audience

Before creating content on LinkedIn, it's essential to have a clear understanding of your target audience. Research their demographics, interests, pain points, and preferences. This knowledge will enable you to create content that addresses their needs, interests, and challenges effectively. Tailoring your content to resonate with your audience increases the likelihood of engagement, encourages sharing, and positions you as a valuable resource.

Developing a Content Strategy

A well-defined content strategy is crucial for consistency and effectiveness. Determine your goals, whether it's increasing brand awareness, generating leads, or establishing thought leadership.

Identify the topics and themes that align with your expertise and target audience's interests. Plan the frequency and types of content you will create, such as articles, videos, infographics, or industry insights. A content strategy ensures that your content is purposeful, cohesive, and aligned with your business objectives.

Crafting Compelling Headlines

The headline is the first impression your content makes, and a compelling headline can significantly impact whether someone clicks to read further. Craft headlines that are concise, attention-grabbing, and clearly communicate the value proposition of your content. Use powerful words, ask thought-provoking questions, or promise valuable insights to entice readers to engage with your content. A strong headline sets the tone for your content and encourages readers to delve deeper.

Writing Engaging Articles and Posts

When creating content on LinkedIn, it's essential to focus on quality and relevance. Whether you write articles or make posts, here are some tips to make your content engaging:

1. *Provide Value:* Your content should offer valuable insights, actionable advice, or industry knowledge. Solve problems, answer common questions, or share your expertise. When your audience finds value in your content, they are more likely to engage, comment, and share it with others.
2. *Be Authentic:* Inject your personality and unique perspective into your content. Authenticity helps you connect with your audience on a deeper level. Share personal stories, lessons learned, or anecdotes that resonate with your audience's experiences. This humanizes your brand and fosters a sense of trust and relatability.
3. *Use Visuals:* Incorporate visual elements such as images, infographics, or videos to make your content visually appealing and easily digestible. Visuals grab attention, break up text, and enhance the overall engagement of your content.

4. *Encourage Conversation:* Pose questions, seek opinions, or invite readers to share their experiences in the comments section. Encouraging conversation sparks engagement and fosters a sense of community around your content. Respond to comments promptly and engage in meaningful discussions to further build connections.
5. *Optimize for Readability:* Structure your content using subheadings, bullet points, and paragraphs for easy skimming. Use concise sentences and avoid jargon or overly technical language. Make your content accessible and engaging to a wide range of readers.

Leveraging Native Video Content

Native video content on LinkedIn has gained significant traction in recent years. Utilize this powerful medium to create engaging videos that resonate with your audience. Consider the following tips:

1. *Keep it Short and Engaging:* Attention spans are limited, so keep your videos concise and focused. Deliver your message within the first few seconds to capture attention and maintain interest throughout the video.
2. *Provide Value:* Just like written content, ensure your video offers value to your audience. Educate, entertain, or inspire them with actionable insights, tips, or stories. Make it worth their time investment.
3. *Include Captions:* Many users watch videos without sound, so adding captions ensures your message is accessible and effectively conveyed. Captions also make your video more engaging for viewers who prefer to read the content.
4. *Call to Action:* End your video with a clear call to action. Whether it's directing viewers to your website, subscribing to your newsletter, or engaging in further conversation, guide them on the next step they should take.

Engaging with Other Content

Building a presence on LinkedIn is not just about creating your own content; it's also about engaging with others' content. Actively participate in discussions, like, comment, and share relevant content within your industry. Engaging with others demonstrates your thoughtfulness, expands your network, and builds relationships with fellow professionals. By providing valuable insights and contributing to conversations, you establish yourself as a trusted and knowledgeable resource.

Creating engaging content on LinkedIn requires a strategic approach and a deep understanding of your target audience. Craft compelling headlines, deliver valuable insights, leverage visual elements, and engage in conversations to foster connections and establish your expertise. By consistently delivering high-quality content, you can grow your audience, increase visibility, and drive meaningful business outcomes.

5

Leveraging LinkedIn Groups for Business Success

LinkedIn Groups provide a powerful platform for professionals to connect, engage, and collaborate within specific industries, interests, or communities. In Chapter 5, we will explore the benefits and strategies of leveraging LinkedIn Groups to enhance your business success. By actively participating in relevant groups, you can expand your network, establish your expertise, generate leads, and foster valuable relationships.

Finding Relevant Groups

The first step in leveraging LinkedIn Groups is to find those that align with your industry, interests, and target audience. Search for groups using relevant keywords and filters to narrow down the results. Look for active groups with a substantial number of members and engaging discussions. Consider joining both industry-specific groups and broader professional communities that attract your target audience. By finding the right groups, you can connect with like- minded professionals and expand your reach within your niche.

Engaging in Meaningful Discussions

Once you've joined relevant LinkedIn Groups, it's crucial to actively engage in meaningful discussions. Look for discussions that align with your expertise or topics you're passionate about. Share your insights, offer advice, and contribute valuable information to the conversation. By providing helpful and relevant input, you establish yourself as a knowledgeable professional and gain visibility within the group. Engaging in discussions also allows you to learn from others, gain new perspectives, and stay updated on industry trends.

Sharing Valuable Content

LinkedIn Groups provide an excellent opportunity to share your content and establish yourself as a thought leader. Create and share valuable articles, blog posts, videos, or infographics that resonate with the group members. Ensure your content provides valuable insights, actionable tips, or industry knowledge. Be mindful of the group's rules and guidelines regarding self-promotion, and focus on delivering value rather than blatant advertising. When group members find your content helpful, they are more likely to engage with it, share it, and view you as a trusted resource.

Initiating Discussions

Don't just wait for discussions to happen; take the initiative to start conversations within the LinkedIn Groups. Pose thought-provoking questions, seek opinions on industry-related topics, or share interesting news or articles. By initiating discussions, you encourage engagement and foster a sense of community within the group. Be responsive to the comments and insights shared by other members to maintain an active and engaging discussion. Initiating discussions positions you as a leader and facilitator within the group.

Building Relationships

LinkedIn Groups offer a unique opportunity to build valuable relationships with professionals in your industry or target audience. Engage with group members by liking, commenting, and sharing their posts. Acknowledge their contributions, offer support, and provide thoughtful feedback. Actively participate in discussions started by other group members and connect with those who share common interests or goals. When you build meaningful relationships within the group, you expand your network and open doors for collaboration, referrals, and business opportunities.

Establishing Your Expertise

Consistently engaging in LinkedIn Groups helps establish your expertise and credibility within your industry. When you consistently share valuable insights, participate in discussions, and provide helpful information, group members will recognize you as a knowledgeable professional. This recognition can lead to opportunities such as speaking engagements, guest blogging, or industry partnerships. Establishing your expertise through LinkedIn Groups enhances your personal brand and positions you as a trusted authority in your field.

Leveraging Group Events and Announcements

LinkedIn Groups often host events, webinars, or virtual conferences. Take advantage of these opportunities to attend, participate, or even present. Group events allow you to network with fellow professionals, learn from industry experts, and showcase your knowledge and skills. Additionally, leverage group announcements to share relevant updates, product launches, or company news. Group members who are interested in your offerings or industry-related updates can connect with you, leading to potential business opportunities or partnerships.

Monitoring Group Analytics

LinkedIn provides group analytics that give insights into the performance of your group activities. Monitor the analytics to understand which discussions or content resonate the most with group members. Identify the most engaged members and nurture those relationships further. Pay attention to the topics that generate the most interest and tailor your future content and discussions accordingly. Monitoring group analytics helps you refine your LinkedIn Group strategy and maximize your impact within the community.

Leveraging LinkedIn Groups is a powerful way to expand your network, establish your expertise, and foster valuable relationships. Engage in meaningful discussions, share valuable content, initiate conversations, and build relationships within the groups. By actively participating and providing value, you position yourself as a trusted resource and open doors for business growth and collaboration.

6

Expanding Your Reach with LinkedIn Ads

LinkedIn Ads offer a targeted and effective way to expand your reach, increase brand visibility, and generate leads on the platform. In Chapter 6, we will explore the strategies and techniques for leveraging LinkedIn Ads to achieve your business goals. By understanding the different ad formats, targeting options, and optimization strategies, you can maximize the impact of your advertising campaigns and reach a relevant audience of professionals.

Understanding LinkedIn Ad Formats

LinkedIn offers various ad formats to suit different marketing objectives and budgets. Familiarize yourself with the available ad formats, including:

1. *Sponsored Content:* These ads appear directly in the LinkedIn feed and blend seamlessly with organic content. Sponsored Content allows you to promote articles, videos, or other engaging content to a targeted audience.
2. *Sponsored InMail:* This format allows you to send personalized messages directly to the LinkedIn inboxes of your target audience. Sponsored InMail enables you to deliver targeted messages, such as event invitations, product announcements, or personalized offers.
3. *Text Ads:* These are small, text-based ads that appear on the right- hand side or top

of LinkedIn pages. Text Ads are cost-effective and can be used to drive traffic to your LinkedIn profile, website, or landing pages.

4. *Dynamic Ads:* Dynamic Ads are personalized ads that use LinkedIn member profile data to deliver highly relevant and personalized messages. They can include profile pictures, job titles, or other information to capture attention and drive engagement.

Defining Your Advertising Goals

Before launching a LinkedIn Ads campaign, it's essential to define your advertising goals. Consider whether you want to increase brand awareness, drive website traffic, generate leads, or promote specific products or services. Clearly defining your goals will guide your ad creation, targeting, and optimization strategies. Each goal requires a different approach, so be specific and measurable in determining your desired outcomes.

Targeting the Right Audience

One of the key advantages of LinkedIn Ads is its powerful targeting options. Use the available targeting criteria to narrow down your audience based on factors such as job title, industry, company size, location, and more. Refine your audience by considering their interests, skills, or groups they are part of. By precisely targeting your ads, you can reach the professionals who are most likely to be interested in your offerings, increasing the effectiveness of your campaigns.

Crafting Compelling Ad Copy and Visuals

Captivating ad copy and visuals are essential for grabbing attention and driving engagement. Write clear, concise, and compelling ad copy that communicates the value proposition of your offerings.

Highlight the benefits, address pain points, and use persuasive language to entice your audience to take action. Use eye-catching visuals, such as high-quality images or videos, that are relevant to your message. Ensure that your ad copy and visuals align with your brand voice and resonate with your target audience.

Implementing Conversion Tracking

To measure the success of your LinkedIn Ads campaigns, it's crucial to implement conversion tracking. Set up conversion tracking pixels on your website or landing pages to track actions such as form submissions, purchases, or downloads. By tracking conversions, you can analyze the effectiveness of your ads, optimize your targeting and messaging, and make data-driven decisions to improve your campaign performance.

Testing and Optimization

To maximize the effectiveness of your LinkedIn Ads, continuous testing and optimization are key. Experiment with different ad formats, headlines, visuals, and targeting options to identify what resonates best with your audience. A/B test different elements of your ads, such as call-to-action buttons or ad placements, to determine the most effective combinations. Monitor the performance metrics, such as click-through rates, conversion rates, and cost per click, and make adjustments accordingly. Optimization is an ongoing process that allows you to refine your campaigns and achieve better results over time.

Setting a Budget and Monitoring Results

When running LinkedIn Ads, it's important to set a budget that aligns with your advertising goals and overall marketing budget. Determine how much you're willing to spend daily or over the duration of your campaign. Monitor your ad spend and performance metrics regularly to ensure you stay within budget and achieve your desired results.

Use the analytics and reporting features provided by LinkedIn Ads to gain insights into your campaign performance, understand the return on investment, and make informed decisions for future campaigns.

Expanding your reach on LinkedIn through targeted advertising can significantly enhance your brand visibility, lead generation efforts, and overall business growth. Understand the available ad formats, define your goals, target the right audience, craft compelling ad copy and visuals, and implement conversion tracking. Continuously test, optimize, and monitor your campaigns to maximize the impact of your LinkedIn Ads and achieve your desired outcomes.

7

Building Your Personal Brand on LinkedIn

In today's professional landscape, building a strong personal brand is essential for career advancement and business success. LinkedIn provides a powerful platform to showcase your expertise, connect with professionals, and establish yourself as a thought leader. In Chapter 7, we will delve into the strategies and techniques for building a compelling personal brand on LinkedIn. By optimizing your profile, sharing valuable content, engaging with your network, and leveraging LinkedIn features, you can create a strong and influential presence on the platform.

Optimizing Your Profile

Your LinkedIn profile is the foundation of your personal brand on the platform. Optimize your profile to make a strong first impression and highlight your professional achievements. Here are key elements to focus on:

1. *Professional Headline:* Craft a concise and attention-grabbing headline that showcases your expertise and unique value proposition.
2. *Profile Picture:* Choose a professional and high-quality profile picture that represents your personal brand and creates a positive impression.
3. *About Section:* Craft a compelling summary that highlights your skills, experience, and career accomplishments. Use keywords

relevant to your industry to optimize your profile for search.

4. *Experience and Education:* Provide detailed information about your work experience and education, emphasizing key achievements and responsibilities.
5. *Skills and Endorsements:* List relevant skills and seek endorsements from colleagues and connections to showcase your expertise.

Sharing Valuable Content

Sharing valuable content is a powerful way to establish yourself as a thought leader and engage with your network on LinkedIn. Create and curate content that is relevant to your industry, interests, and target audience. Here's how to do it effectively:

1. *Original Content:* Share your expertise by creating original articles, blog posts, or videos that provide valuable insights, actionable tips, or thought-provoking ideas.

2. *Curated Content:* Share relevant industry news, articles, or reports from reputable sources, accompanied by your insights or comments to add value to the content.
3. *Visual Content:* Leverage visual elements such as infographics, images, or videos to make your content more engaging and shareable.
4. *Consistency:* Maintain a consistent posting schedule to stay top of mind with your network. Aim for a balance between quality and frequency.

Engaging with Your Network

Engagement is key to building relationships and growing your personal brand on LinkedIn. Actively participate in discussions, comment on posts, and respond to comments on your own content. Here are some tips for effective engagement:

1. *Thoughtful Comments:* Leave insightful and thoughtful comments on posts by oth-

ers. Add value to the conversation and spark meaningful discussions.

2. *Networking:* Connect with professionals in your industry, colleagues, and thought leaders. Personalize your connection requests to foster a genuine connection.
3. *Responding to Messages:* Promptly respond to messages and inquiries to show professionalism and build relationships.
4. *Recommendations and Endorsements:* Give and receive recommendations and endorsements to showcase your expertise and build social proof.

Leveraging LinkedIn Features

LinkedIn offers several features that can enhance your personal brand and expand your reach. Familiarize yourself with these features and utilize them strategically:

1. *LinkedIn Articles:* Publish long-form articles on LinkedIn to share in-depth insights, showcase your expertise, and gain visibility.

2. *LinkedIn Live:* Take advantage of the LinkedIn Live feature to host live video broadcasts, interviews, or webinars. It allows you to engage with your audience in real-time and establish yourself as an expert in your field.
3. *LinkedIn Groups:* Join and actively participate in relevant LinkedIn Groups to connect with professionals, engage in industry-specific discussions, and expand your network.
4. *LinkedIn Events:* Utilize the LinkedIn Events feature to promote and organize virtual or in-person events. It helps you reach a targeted audience and generate interest in your offerings.

Seeking Recommendations and Endorsements

Recommendations and endorsements play a crucial role in building credibility and trust on LinkedIn. Request recommendations from colleagues, clients, or partners who can speak to your skills and work ethic. Seek endorsements for your key skills to highlight your expertise and reinforce your personal brand.

Monitoring and Adjusting Your Personal Brand Strategy

Building a personal brand is an ongoing process, and it's essential to monitor your efforts and adjust your strategy as needed. Regularly review your LinkedIn analytics to gain insights into the performance of your posts, engagement levels, and overall profile visibility. Assess the type of content that resonates most with your audience and adjust your content strategy accordingly. Continuously refine your personal brand to align with your professional goals and the evolving needs of your target audience.

By implementing these strategies, you can build a powerful personal brand on LinkedIn that attracts opportunities, establishes your expertise, and fosters valuable connections.

8

Utilizing LinkedIn Analytics for Data Insights

LinkedIn provides a robust analytics platform that offers valuable insights into the performance of your profile, content, and engagement. In Chapter 8, we will explore how to effectively utilize LinkedIn Analytics to gain data-driven insights and optimize your LinkedIn marketing efforts. By understanding the key metrics, tracking your performance, and leveraging the analytics features, you can make informed decisions to enhance your presence on the platform and achieve your marketing goals.

Key Metrics to Track

Before diving into LinkedIn Analytics, it's important to understand the key metrics that provide insights into your performance. Here are some metrics to track:

1. *Profile Views:* Measure the number of times your profile has been viewed to understand your visibility and reach.
2. *Post Impressions:* Track the number of times your posts have been displayed to gain insights into their reach and potential impact.
3. *Engagement Rate:* Calculate the percentage of people who engaged with your content (likes, comments, shares) compared to the number of impressions to evaluate the effectiveness of your content.
4. *Follower Growth:* Monitor the growth of your followers over time to understand the

impact of your content and engagement strategies.

5. *Click-Through Rate (CTR):* Measure the percentage of people who clicked on a link or CTA in your posts or ads to assess their effectiveness in driving traffic.

Accessing LinkedIn Analytics

LinkedIn Analytics can be accessed through the "My Network" tab on your LinkedIn homepage. Click on "Connections" and then select "Analytics" to access the analytics dashboard. The dashboard provides an overview of your profile, content, and audience metrics, allowing you to gain a comprehensive understanding of your LinkedIn performance.

Analyzing Profile Metrics

The profile metrics section in LinkedIn Analytics provides valuable insights into your profile's visibility and impact. Monitor metrics such as profile views, search appearances, and connections to understand how your profile is performing. Identify trends and patterns to optimize your profile and increase your visibility among your target audience. Regularly update your profile with relevant information, keywords, and engaging content to improve your profile metrics.

Tracking Content Performance

LinkedIn Analytics offers insights into the performance of your content, helping you understand what resonates with your audience and drives engagement. Analyze metrics such as post impressions, engagement rate, clicks, and shares to identify your top-performing content. Evaluate the topics, formats, and strategies that generate the highest engagement and replicate those in future content creation. Experiment with different types of content, such as articles, videos, or infographics, and track their performance to refine your content strategy.

Understanding Audience Insights

Audience insights provide valuable information about your LinkedIn followers, helping you tailor your content and engagement strategies. LinkedIn Analytics offers demographic data such as location, industry, job titles, and seniority of your followers. Use these insights to understand your target audience better and create content that addresses their needs and interests. Adapt your messaging, tone, and content formats to resonate with your specific audience segments.

Tracking Ad Performance

If you are running LinkedIn Ads, the analytics dashboard provides data on ad performance, including impressions, clicks, and conversion rates. Monitor these metrics to assess the effectiveness of your ads and make data-driven optimizations. Test different ad formats, targeting options, and messaging variations to find the best-

performing combinations. Regularly review your ad analytics to refine your ad strategy and maximize your return on investment.

Using Insights for Optimization

LinkedIn Analytics empowers you to make data-driven decisions and optimize your LinkedIn marketing efforts. Use the insights gathered from profile metrics, content performance, audience data, and ad analytics to refine your strategy. Identify trends, patterns, and areas for improvement, and adjust your content, engagement, and targeting strategies accordingly. Regularly track your metrics, set goals, and measure your progress to continually improve your performance on LinkedIn.

By leveraging LinkedIn Analytics effectively, you can gain valuable insights into your profile, content, audience, and ad performance. These insights enable you to optimize your LinkedIn marketing strategy, improve engagement, and achieve your marketing objectives on the platform.

9

Maximizing LinkedIn Recommendations

LinkedIn recommendations and endorsements play a vital role in building credibility, trust, and a strong personal brand on the platform. In Chapter 9, we will explore strategies for maximizing the power of LinkedIn recommendations and endorsements. By actively seeking recommendations, giving endorsements, and leveraging these features effectively, you can enhance your professional reputation, strengthen your network, and attract new opportunities.

The Importance of Recommendations and Endorsements

Recommendations and endorsements on LinkedIn serve as social proof of your skills, expertise, and professional character. They provide validation from colleagues, clients, and other connections, enhancing your credibility and trustworthiness. Recommendations offer detailed testimonials that highlight your strengths, while endorsements validate your skills with a simple click. These features significantly impact how others perceive you and can influence their decision to connect, hire, or collaborate with you.

Seeking Recommendations

Actively seeking recommendations is an effective way to showcase your expertise and build a strong personal brand on LinkedIn. Here are some strategies to maximize your recommendations:

1. *Identify Relevant Contacts:* Consider individuals who have worked closely with you and can speak to your skills, work ethic, and accomplishments. This may include colleagues, supervisors, clients, or partners.
2. *Personalize Your Request:* When reaching out for a recommendation, personalize your message to provide context and remind the person of your collaboration or working relationship. Clearly explain why you value their opinion and how their recommendation will benefit both parties.
3. *Provide Guidance:* To make it easier for the person writing the recommendation, provide specific guidance on the key areas you would like them to focus on. For example, you can suggest highlighting specific projects, skills, or qualities that you would like to showcase.
4. *Follow Up and Express Gratitude:* Once you receive a recommendation, express your gratitude by sending a personalized thank-you message. Building and maintain-

ing strong relationships is essential for long-term success on LinkedIn.

Giving Thoughtful Endorsements

Endorsements are a quick and easy way to validate someone's skills and contribute to their professional reputation. Here's how to give thoughtful endorsements:

1. *Be Genuine:* Only endorse someone for skills you have personally observed or experienced. Endorsements should reflect your honest opinion and be based on your first-hand knowledge of the person's abilities.
2. *Select Relevant Skills:* Focus on endorsing skills that are relevant to the person's professional goals and expertise. This ensures that your endorsements are meaningful and align with their personal brand.
3. *Provide Context:* When endorsing someone, consider adding a brief note or comment to provide context and highlight specific examples of their skills in action.

This adds value to your endorsement and makes it more impactful.

4. *Engage in Reciprocal Endorsements:* Consider endorsing professionals in your network who have endorsed you. Reciprocal endorsements strengthen professional relationships and demonstrate your willingness to support others.

Displaying Recommendations and Endorsements

To maximize the impact of recommendations and endorsements, ensure they are prominently displayed on your LinkedIn profile.

Here's how to showcase them effectively:

1. *Arrange Recommendations Strategically:* Organize your recommendations to highlight the most relevant and impressive ones. Feature those from influential individuals or high-profile clients at the top of your recommendations section.
2. *Highlight Key Skills:* LinkedIn allows you to select up to 50 skills to display on your

profile. Choose skills that are most relevant to your personal brand and showcase the ones with the highest number of endorsements.

3. *Request LinkedIn Recommendations from Colleagues:* You can ask for recommendations directly from your connections using LinkedIn's built-in recommendation request feature. This makes it convenient for your contacts to provide recommendations and ensures they appear on your profile.

Engaging with Recommendations and Endorsements

Engagement is crucial when it comes to recommendations and endorsements on LinkedIn. Show appreciation to those who provide recommendations or endorsements by liking, commenting, or sending a personalized message to express your gratitude. Engage with their content, provide support, and maintain strong relationships within your network.

Leveraging Recommendations and Endorsements for Networking and Job Opportunities

LinkedIn recommendations and endorsements not only strengthen your personal brand but also open doors to networking and job opportunities. Here's how to leverage them effectively:

1. *Share Recommendations on Other Platforms:* If appropriate, showcase your LinkedIn recommendations on other professional platforms, such as your personal website or online portfolio. This demonstrates the positive feedback you have received and boosts your credibility beyond the LinkedIn platform.
2. *Utilize Recommendations in Job Applications:* When applying for job positions, include select recommendations that align with the requirements of the role. This provides hiring managers with additional insights into your skills and work ethic.
3. *Leverage Recommendations for Networking:* Share relevant recommendations when

reaching out to new contacts or when attending networking events. This helps establish credibility and trust from the outset, making it more likely for others to engage and connect with you.

4. *Provide Recommendations and Endorsements to Others:* Show support for your connections by providing recommendations and endorsements to deserving individuals in your network. This helps foster mutually beneficial relationships and encourages others to reciprocate.

By actively seeking recommendations, giving thoughtful endorsements, and leveraging these features strategically, you can maximize their impact on your personal brand, networking efforts, and job opportunities.

10

Expanding Your Business Opportunities on LinkedIn

LinkedIn offers immense potential for expanding your business opportunities and reaching new clients, customers, and partners. In Chapter 10, we will explore strategies to leverage LinkedIn for business growth. By optimizing your profile, building valuable connections, utilizing

LinkedIn's features, and engaging with your audience, you can maximize your chances of success and unlock new business opportunities.

Optimizing Your LinkedIn Profile for Business Growth

Your LinkedIn profile serves as your professional online presence and plays a crucial role in attracting business opportunities. Here are some strategies to optimize your profile:

1. *Craft a Compelling Headline:* Use a concise and engaging headline that highlights your unique value proposition and resonates with your target audience. Clearly communicate what you do and how you can help potential clients or partners.
2. *Showcase Your Expertise:* Utilize the Summary and Experience sections to highlight your skills, achievements, and relevant experience. Use keywords strategically to improve your profile's visibility in LinkedIn searches.

3. *Incorporate Media and Visuals:* Enhance your profile with multimedia elements, such as videos, presentations, or portfolio samples, to showcase your work and capture the attention of visitors.
4. *Request Recommendations:* Gather recommendations from satisfied clients, partners, or colleagues to provide social proof of your expertise and build credibility.

Building Valuable Connections

Expanding your network is key to unlocking business opportunities on LinkedIn. Here are strategies to build valuable connections:

1. *Identify and Connect with Targeted Individuals:* Use LinkedIn's advanced search filters to identify individuals who align with your target audience, potential clients, or industry influencers. Send personalized connection requests to establish meaningful connections.
2. *Engage in Groups and Communities:* Join relevant LinkedIn groups and communities

where your target audience or industry professionals gather. Contribute valuable insights, participate in discussions, and build relationships with like-minded individuals.

3. *Attend and Engage with Events:* Take advantage of LinkedIn Events to discover virtual or in-person industry events. Engage with event attendees, speakers, and organizers to expand your network and create new business opportunities.
4. *Leverage Your Existing Network:* Tap into your existing contacts, such as clients, colleagues, and friends, to expand your network. Ask for introductions or recommendations to reach individuals who may be interested in your products or services.

Utilizing LinkedIn Features for Business Growth

LinkedIn offers various features that can be leveraged to expand your business opportunities. Here are a few key features:

1. *LinkedIn Pages:* Create a LinkedIn Page for your business to showcase your products, services, and company updates. Regularly share valuable content and engage with your followers to build brand awareness and attract potential clients.
2. *LinkedIn Sales Navigator:* Consider using LinkedIn Sales Navigator, a premium feature that provides advanced search and lead generation capabilities. It allows you to identify and engage with potential leads and prospects more effectively.
3. *Sponsored Content and LinkedIn Ads:* Explore sponsored content and LinkedIn Ads to reach a wider audience and promote your products or services. Utilize LinkedIn's targeting options to ensure your ads are seen by the right people.
4. *LinkedIn Messaging and InMail:* Leverage LinkedIn's messaging and InMail features to connect with potential clients, partners, or industry influencers directly. Craft personalized messages that demonstrate your

value and establish meaningful connections.

Engaging with Your Audience

Engagement is key to building relationships and nurturing business opportunities on LinkedIn. Here's how to engage effectively:

1. *Share Valuable Content:* Consistently share valuable and relevant content that educates, entertains, or solves problems for your target audience. Encourage conversations, respond to comments, and actively engage with your audience.
2. *Participate in Discussions:* Engage in discussions within LinkedIn groups, industry forums, or comment sections of relevant posts. Provide insightful contributions, answer questions, and establish yourself as a trusted authority in your field.
3. *Utilize LinkedIn Live:* Consider utilizing LinkedIn Live to host live webinars, Q&A sessions, or product demonstrations. Live video allows you to interact with your au-

dience in real-time and build stronger connections.

4. *Personalize Your Interactions:* When connecting or engaging with potential clients or partners, personalize your messages and interactions. Show genuine interest, ask thoughtful questions, and tailor your communication to their specific needs.

CONCLUSION

LinkedIn presents abundant opportunities for expanding your business reach and attracting new clients, customers, and partners. By optimizing your profile, building valuable connections, utilizing LinkedIn features, and engaging with your audience, you can maximize your business opportunities and achieve sustainable growth.

www.ingramcontent.com/pod-product-compliance
Lightning Source LLC
LaVergne TN
LVHW022022200926
848481LV00007B/2497
9798349526350